Reactions

A workbook to help young people who are experiencing trauma and grief

By Alison Salloum, BCSW

Design by New Idea Design

Revised 2021

ISBN: 978-1-56123-108-9
San: 298-1815

www.centering.org

Email: orders@centeringresources.com

Phone: 1-866-218-0101

CENTERING
AND
GRIEF DIGEST MAGAZINE
GRIEF RESOURCES

To the young person...

When someone close to you dies suddenly, or when you or someone else gets hurt, like shot or stabbed, you may experience different reactions.

Reactions occur because of what has happened. There are emotional reactions, body reactions and behavioral reactions. Emotional reactions are your feelings. Physical reactions are when your body responds to what has happened, and behavioral reactions are how you act because of what has happened.

These reactions may feel very scary, but they are normal when someone gets hurt or killed. This book will help you understand your reactions and make them not happen as much. Sometimes you may feel out of control, but you can have more control over your reactions if you work on it.

Take your time with this book. Only complete 3 to 5 pages at a time and then stop. If you need more room to write or draw there are extra pages in the back of the book. Also, it is recommended that you read and do the worksheets with someone you feel safe with such as a parent, teacher or counselor.

This book belongs to :

To the adult working with the young person...

This book is intended to help children and youth understand and reduce their overwhelming grief and traumatic reactions. It is for children and youth who have witnessed or know someone close to them who has been hurt or killed by violence or who themselves have been a victim of violence. However, this book may be used to help young people work through any type of tragic loss.

It is important that the young person works at their own pace with this book and with a supportive person. It is recommended that only three to five pages are completed at a time, for only about one to two hours a week.

This workbook may be used with individuals, groups or families. It may be used with ages starting at about nine to adult. Because everyone is so different, it may be used with even younger children, but the facilitator needs to make sure the child understands the worksheets.

Sometimes only one page may be used at a time as a "thought" sheet. The "thought" sheet is used to help the young person explore and express their thoughts and feelings more about the chosen issue. The workbook can be followed in order, or topics can be chosen according to what the child is struggling with at the time. For example, if the child is having difficulty feeling safe, they may want to start with those pages first.

Whatever format is used, it is important to encourage the young person to share their work with someone who they trust. Therefore, before beginning this book, the facilitator needs to establish a caring relationship with the young person. In addition, it is important to identify others in the child/youth's life who cares about them and are willing to listen.

This workbook is dedicated to all the young people in New Orleans, Louisiana who have lost someone due to violence.

Honor those you have lost
by listing their names here:

Supports

It is important to know that you have people who care about you. Everyone needs people to help support them when they are reacting to grief and trauma. Some people who care about you might be family, relatives, church members, neighbors, teachers, friends, God, yourself and counselors.

Write the names of the people who care about you on the lines below. If you want, color the figure so that it looks like one of these people.

_____

_____

_____

_____

_____

Grief and Trauma Reactions

Reactions are how you respond to what has happened. It is how you feel, think and act. When someone close to you gets hurt really bad or dies tragically, you may have different grief and trauma reactions. Grief reactions include your feelings, how your body responds and how you act differently because of what has happened. For example, you may feel sad because they died, or you may start having stomach aches. Trauma reactions occur because of how sudden and/or horrible it was. For example, you may react by trying to avoid the place where it happened or by feeling really jumpy every time you hear a noise.

Many times people try to "just forget about it" or "get over it," but everyone has some type of reaction. You may try to push it away, not talk about it or put it in the back of your mind, but sometimes that will not be possible. You may start to act differently and do things you normally would not do. For example, you may start talking back to people or getting into fights. Most times the reactions will not go away unless you start sharing your thoughts and feelings.

This time can be very scary. To make it not feel so scary, try to talk about your grief and trauma reactions with someone you trust.

Some people ask, "How long will it take for the grief and trauma reactions to go away?" How long do you think? (circle one or write your own answer)

one week   two weeks   three months

six months   one year   two years

Your own answer:

Grief and Trauma

The amount of time that people have reactions from grief and trauma is different for every person. It depends on how close you were to the one who was hurt or killed and what has happened. If someone close to you died, you will never forget that person who died. But it is important to start talking about it so that you do not always feel so sad and/or angry inside.

The reactions will not happen as much if you let yourself talk about what happened and feel the feelings. But it is important to share your thoughts and feelings with someone you feel safe with.

List at least two people who you can talk with and feel safe with:

1. _____

2. _____

What do you think it means to say that you feel safe with someone?

Grief

Grief is the pain caused by the loss and changes. There are many different types of losses. The feelings caused by the loss are different for each person.

Some types of losses are when you leave your friends, when your parents divorce or separate or when one parent leaves the family for good, when a pet dies, or when a person dies. Can you list any other types of losses?

_____

_____

_____

_____

In the beginning, the grief may feel like it will never go away. For a while the grief will come and go. Some days you may not have too much grief and you feel calm. On other days, the grief may feel like a storm inside you.

How has it been for you today? (circle one)

calm   stormy   both

Eventually, there will be more calm days than stormy days, but only if you ride out the storm. In other words, if you have stormy days (or days when you are grieving a lot) and pretend that the grief is not there, it will only come back another day. But if you recognize the grief (the storm), it will go away. Soon you will feel better. The grief will not come back as much, and it won't feel so bad when it does.

If you let yourself experience the grief, you will eventually feel better.

Grief

There will be...

stormy days
a lot of grief.

cloudy days
some grief

calm days
little grief

sunny days
no grief

Some days it will be stormy, cloudy, calm and sunny all in the same day.

Draw how your grief feels today...

Shock

When grief and/or trauma happens, you may go into SHOCK.

You may say, "I cannot believe it happened."
You may not think or do anything.

After the Shock, you may start to DENY IT.

You may say, "It did not really happen.
It is not for real.
Everything is the same."

You may feel NUMB.

You may not know how you feel or what you think.

Are you still in shock? (circle one)   Yes   No   Sometimes

Do you still deny that it happened? (circle one)   Yes   No   Sometimes

Do you feel numb? (circle one)   Yes   No   Sometimes

Remember as you start this book, everyone has different reactions. No one is ever exactly the same. It is important to find out how you are REACTING to what has happened. It is important to begin by explaining and talking about what actually happened. Go to the next page and try.

write or draw about
what happened...

Write or draw about what was the
worst moment for you...

Feelings

During this time, you may have many different feelings. Because so much has happened, you might not know how you feel or you may feel overwhelmed by your feelings. Talking about your feelings can help.
Cut the feeling cards out and talk about a time when you felt that feeling. Afterwards, use the cards to play feeling charades. Or make up your own games with the cards!!

To play feeling charades, pass out all the cards. Act out the feeling card you have in your hand and have others guess what card you have.

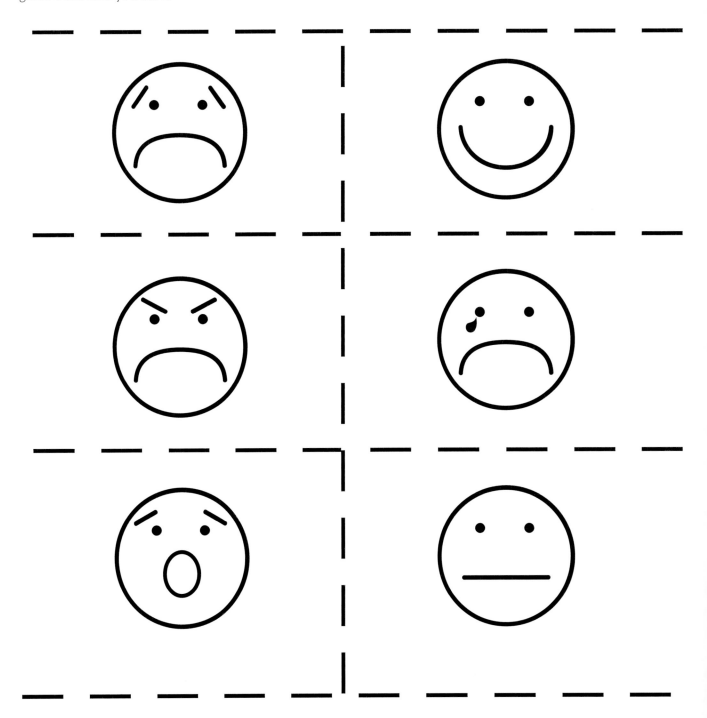

Feelings

Try to complete these sentences. Describe how you felt or are feeling.

When this terrible thing happened, I first felt _____.

Lately, I have mostly felt _____.

When I think about what happened, I feel _____

and _____.

A feeling that I have a hard time showing others is _____.

I feel worried because _____.

When I get nervous, others can tell because I _____.

I feel guilty because_____.

I feel most afraid when _____.

Sometimes I feel jealous because _____.

One thing that makes me happy is _____.

Feelings

How much do you feel these feelings lately?

None   A little   Some   Much   Most

complete the following sentences by using the words above. Draw whatever feeling faces you want to in the circles.

Lately, I feel happy _____ of the time.

Lately, I feel angry _____ of the time.

Lately, I feel sad _____ of the time.

Lately, I feel lonely _____ of the time.

Lately, I feel nervous _____ of the time.

Lately, I feel helpless _____ of the time.

Lately, I feel guilty _____ of the time.

Lately, I feel scared _____ of the time.

Lately, I feel jealous _____ of the time.

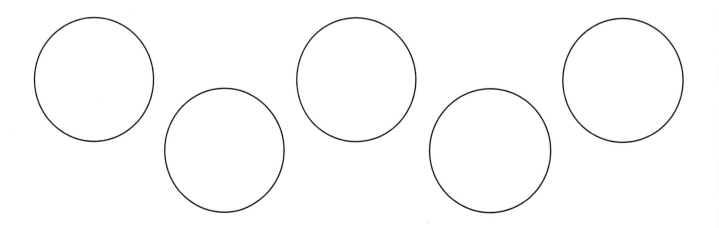

Anger

When you or someone you care about gets hurt or killed, there is usually a time when you start feeling angry. This may be right after it happened or it may be sometime afterwards. Sometimes, people get a "I don't care" attitude. Most times this means "I am angry".

It is hard for many people to say why they are feeling angry. It can be even harder to know what to do with the feelings of anger. Because of ange, people act in ways that lead to trouble. To begin to manage your anger better, start with writing below whatever comes to mind. Do not worry about what you write or how you spell.

When I think about what happened, I get angry because...

When you get really angry, have you noticed any reactions that happen to your body? (check)

- ◯ I start to sweat
- ◯ My heart starts racing
- ◯ My fists shut tight
- ◯ I bite down on my teeth
- ◯ I get a headache
- ◯ My face or body feels hot

If you have checked one or more reactions, that is good because you can use these reactions to let yourself know that you are really angry. These reactions are "signs" of your anger.

Being able to recognize your anger reactions can be an alarm system to yourself to STOP and THINK before you ACT OUT YOUR ANGER.

Anger

Sometimes when people feel angry they DISPLACE it. This means that they take their anger out on people they are not really angry with. It is easier to act mad at them than face what they're really angry about. Instead of getting angry about what has happened, you may get angry at someone else.

For example: Terrell was angry because his family took down all the photographs of his brother who died. He was really mad at his family but could not tell them that he felt angry because the photographs were taken down. Terrell went to school and displaced his anger on his teacher. He would not do anything that his teacher asked him to do and he started yelling back at his teacher.

What could Terrell have done instead?

_____

_____

_____

_____

_____

When you feel angry with someone, it is good to ask yourself, "Are you really angry at them or are you upset because of something else? Who or what are you feeling angry about?"

Tell about a time when you DISPLACED your anger on someone.

_____

_____

_____

_____

_____

_____

Anger

When you feel angry it is a good idea to try to actively do something. Put a check by the ones you have tried. Put a star by one that you will try next time you feel angry.

Say "I am angry because_____."

Count to ten backwards...10.　　9.　　8.　　7.　　6.　　5.　　4.　　3.　　2.　　1.

Take three deep breaths...　　1...　　2...　　3...

Realize you are angry and just sit with your feeling.

Go play a sport.

Go for a walk or run.

Write in your journal how you are feeling.

Draw really fast how you are feeling – then tear it up.

Talk with someone who listens to you and tell them how you feel.

Look up in the sky and say to yourself "I need to calm down."

Scream into a pillow.

Listen to music that expresses how you are feeling.

Write other things you do to manage your anger:

1. _____

2. _____

Guilt

It is normal to think of ways you could have stopped it from happening. However, when someone gets hurt or dies because of violence, the only one who is at fault is the one who did the violent act.

You might have thoughts like "What if I had asked him to stay home: then he wouldn't have been killed," or "What if I had been nicer to them then they would not have gone outside and been stabbed" or " If only I had been there, I could have stopped her from being shot."

You might have "what if…" thoughts, but the truth is, if you are not the one that killed the person, then it is not your fault. It is also important to know that thoughts cannot kill someone. For example, if you said, "I wish you were dead," and later that week they got killed, your thoughts did not kill that person. The bullet killed him and the person who used the gun killed that person.

Have you had thoughts or dreams about how you could have stopped it or dreams about how you would have done something or not done something to prevent it from happening?

Write or draw about about any of your "what if or If only…" thoughts

Body Reactions

When grief and trauma occurs, your body may react. Common body reactions include:

Stomachaches   Headaches   Tight chest   Heart racing

Sweating   crying   Vomiting   Tired body

Losing or gaining weight

Do you remember any of your body reactions when it first happened?
Write them below:

Did you have any of these body reactions right after or a few days after it happened?
If yes, write which ones:

In the last two weeks, have you had any of these body reactions occur? (circle one)

Yes   No

If yes, write which ones:

How often would you say these body reactions occur? (circle one)

once a week   twice a week   three times a week   almost every day

Body Reactions

It is important to take extra care of your body during this time. These are some ways to take care of your body's needs:

Eat healthy food (include fruits and vegetables)

Exercise every day (Play sports, ride your bike, go for a walk)

Take deep breaths at least five times a day

Get eight hours of sleep a night

Take a warm bath

Listen to calm music

Do something nice for yourself

List other ways to be good to your body:

_____

_____

_____

_____

_____

_____

Behavior Reactions

Because of what has happened, you may start behaving differently. You might not notice it unless others tell you. Try to identify any behavior reactions that have occurred since this happened. Some may be helpful for you, and other actions, such as fighting, may lead to trouble.

Check the behavior reactions you have had since this happened.

I stay by myself more

I spend more time in my room

I want to be around people more now

I sleep with a light on now

I have wet my bed since this happened

I have started getting into fights

I have started talking back to others

I have been smoking more

I started helping my family more

I have not been playing as much as I used to

I cry more. Crying can be both a feeling reaction and a behavior reaction. Some people cry and others do not.

When is the last time you cried?

Have you noticed other ways you have been acting differently? If so, list them below:

_____

_____

_____

_____

Family Reactions

When a family member or friend has been hurt or died, everyone's reactions may be very different. Some will cry, others may not want to talk about it. Other family members may need to talk about it. You may notice that people in your family start acting differently, they are having grief and trauma reactions.

Draw stick people to represent your family and write one thing you have noticed about them since all this happened.

Try to talk with your family about the different feelings, body reactions and behavior reactions that people may have to grief and trauma. You may want to show them this book.

Questioning

This time can be very confusing. You may have many questions you have been wanting to ask someone. For some questions, there may not be any answers, but just asking the questions and talking about them with someone you trust can often help.

Write down any questions you may have.

Cut this out and give it to someone you think will be able to help you. And talk about it.

_____

_____

_____

_____

_____

_____

_____

I want to know...

_____

_____

_____

_____

_____

_____

Life Events

No matter how young or old you are, everyone has had times in their lives that they will never forget. These may be good or bad events and happy or sad times.

1. Write or draw about these things that have happened in your life.
2. Under each box write about how old you were at the time it occurred.

_____ _____

Your Future

When someone gets hurt or dies, you may start thinking about your future. You may think that you will not have a future or that you, too, may die soon.

Before this happened, what were some of your thoughts about your future:

What were your dreams for yourself? What goals did you have? What did you think about doing in the future?

_____

_____

_____

Even though this has happened, you can still work towards your dreams!

What do you need to do or keep doing to help you reach your dreams or goals?

1. _____

2. _____

3. _____

Who in your life can help you to reach your dreams or goals?

1. _____

2. _____

Feeling Jumpy

Sometimes after something really scary happens, people feel like they need to be constantly "on guard". They may be more nervous inside and they might jump if they hear the slightest little noise. They may feel like they have to always watch their back.

While being alert in a violent area is smart, it is good to have some time when you can relax and not feel jumpy or nervous. You need to have a place where you feel safe.

Have you noticed that since this terrible thing happened you feel more "jumpy"? (circle one)

    Yes   No

If yes, how often do you feel this way? (circle one)

a little bit   some of the time   most of the time   all the time

Tell about a time when you felt "jumpy":

_____

_____

_____

_____

_____

_____

_____

It is important to have a time and a place where you can feel relaxed and safe.
Right after completing this page, go to the next page...

Feeling Safe

Feeling safe means feeling good, not scared. It means feeling relaxed, comfortable, not on guard or nervous or jumpy. It is important to know that you can feel safe. If you do not have a place where you feel safe, make up a place that feels safe.

Write or draw about how your safe place looks. Are there any people there? If so, who? What does the area look like? What is the weather like? Do you hear any sounds? What colors are around you? What are you doing? How do you feel?

My Safe Place

After you draw your safe place, talk about it with a safe person. Try and shut your eyes and pretend that you are there. Every time you get that jumpy feeling, shut you eyes and go to your safe place for a minute. This will help you feel more relaxed.

Running Thoughts

Sometimes you may feel like you cannot stop the thoughts about what has happened from replaying over and over in your mind. Sometimes these thoughts come back to you even when you do not want them to. It may seem like a video that keeps rewinding and playing in your head.

Do you ever have thoughts about what happened running on and on in your head?

Yes　　No.　　(circle one)If yes, try to write about these running thoughts:

My Running Thoughts

_____

_____

_____

_____

_____

_____

_____

_____

Do these thoughts scare you or make you feel good?

_____

_____

_____

Review of Reactions

Try to list all the reactions that you have had (or are having) since all this happened. If you are still having any, put a star by them.

Feelings:

_____

_____

_____

_____

_____

Body Reactions:

_____

_____

_____

_____

_____

Behaviors:

_____

_____

_____

_____

_____

Running Thoughts

Try doing the following things to stop the running thoughts:

1. Write down the thoughts.

2. Tell someone you trust about your thoughts.

3. Imagine yourself at your safe place.

4. Every time these thoughts enter your mind, scream inside to yourself "STOP".

5. When you have these thoughts, picture yourself pressing the eject button and the tape coming out. Imagine yourself putting in your favorite video tape or game.

6. When you start to have these thoughts, think about something that makes you happy.

7. When the thoughts enter your mind tell yourself, "I do not have to think about this now."

8. Start doing something you enjoy.

Re-experiencing

Have you ever thought you heard the voice of the person who has died? Have you ever thought you saw that person? Many other people who have had someone close to them die have reported seeing or hearing the person, smelling a familiar smell of that person (like the perfume or cologne they used to wear), and/or thinking that the person is touching them. While this scares some people, it makes others feel good.

Also, some people who have been through a really scary event have said that even after it is over, they have felt like it is happening all over again.

If you have had any experiences like these, write down what happened in the space below:

_____

_____

_____

_____

_____

_____

These experiences make me feel...

_____

_____

_____

_____

_____

Dreams

Draw or write about any dreams or nightmares that you have had since all this happened. If it was a nightmare, write or draw about it and then change the ending so it does not make you feel scared.

My Dream

Avoiding People, Places or Things

Sometimes after something horrible happens there may be certain people, places or things that will remind you about what happened. If this person, place or thing makes you feel upset, you may want to avoid it. For example, after a young boy's brother was shot two streets from his home, he would not go down that street.

Are there any places, people or things that you try to stay away from since this happened? Write or draw about them here:

What do you think would happen if you went near the place, person or thing that you have been trying to avoid?

_____

_____

_____

_____

_____

Avoiding People, Places or Things

When something bad happens, people try to find a reason why it happened. If you cannot think of a certain answer, you may start to make up one. You may think it happened because of a super-natural power or bad luck.

For example: If you put on a new necklace or earring the day you got hurt, you may think the piece of jewelry was bad luck or carried some type of evil spirit. You may start to think the jewelry caused the bad luck.

Another example: A young girl loved playing with dogs. One day she was bitten by her friend's German Shepherd. She decided that all German Shepherds were mean, attack dogs. Every time she saw a German Shepherd, she would run away.

Do you think the jewelry could have had something to do with the person getting hurt?

_____

_____

_____

Does it make sense for the girl to believe that all German Shepherds are mean attack dogs that will hurt her?

_____

_____

_____

Is there any person, place, or thing that you think has "super-natural, evil, or bad power" that caused this to happen? Explain. . .

_____

_____

_____

_____

Avoiding Places, People or Things
My brave plan

On _____ I , _____
NAME THE DAY   YOUR NAME

will try to go near _____
.
PERSON, PLACE OR THING THAT YOU HAVE BEEN STAYING AWAY FROM SINCE THIS TERRIBLE THING HAPPENED

Before I do this, I will talk about it with _____.
NAME SOMEONE YOU TRUST

I will go on my own or with _____.
NAME SOMEONE YOU TRUST

I know that If I need to leave I can and it is okay.

After I have done this, I will talk with _____ about how I felt.
NAME SOMEONE YOU TRUST

I know that working on this brave plan makes me a brave person.

Spirituality

When bad things happen, many people start to question their beliefs. They may start praying more. They may even stop praying because they are angry at God. If someone close to you has died, you may start to wonder what happens to the person after life. There are many beliefs about this and different religions and families teach different things.

However you have responded it is okay, but it is important to talk about it. All kind of questions about God, angels, higher powers, heaven and hell may come to you.

Draw a picture of God or your higher power or what heaven looks like or where the person who has died is now.

When people are grieving their relationship with God may change. Is there someone in your family that you can talk to about this? (circle one)

Yes or no

If yes, who? _____.

If not, try to think about someone you feel close to that you can talk about this with.
Write their name here _____. Talk with them.

You may want to show them this page to help you talk.

Spirituality

Write a special prayer, poem or song, or draw a special picture.

At the end of this book...

See if you know and feel the statements below. Read the "Things I know" certificate out loud to yourself and to someone you trust.

Things I know

I, _____, know more about my reactions to my trauma and grief. I am a very brave person for working in this book and for talking about my reactions. I know that even though this happened, I am okay. I know that I have people who care about me. I know that the world can be violent sometimes, but I can feel safe. My reactions do not happen as much and I feel better. Another thing I know after working in this book is. . .

_____

_____

_____

_____

_____

_____

_____

_____

Signature _____

Date _____